My Day at the Beach

ticktock

Copyright © ticktock Entertainment Ltd 2007
First published in Great Britain in 2007 by ticktock Media Ltd.,
Unit 2, Orchard Business Centre, North Farm Road,
Tunbridge Wells, Kent, TN2 3XF

ticktock project editor: Julia Adams
ticktock project designer: Emma Randall
ticktock picture researcher: Lizzie Knowles

We would like to thank: Jo Hanks, Debra Voege, Colin Beer, Rebecca Clunes

ISBN 978 1 84696 480 0 pbk

Printed in China

Picture credits
t = top, b = bottom, c = centre, l = left, r = right, OFC = outside front cover, OBC = outside back cover

Alamy: 7. Getty Images/ National Geographic: 19b, OBCbr. Image Source: 8, 9, 10l, 11, 13, 14, 15r
OBCcr. Jupiter Images/Image 100: OFCr. Photolibrary: 18t. Shutterstock: 1, 5, 8-9 background, 12, 16,
17bl, 21, 23. Superstock: 4, 6, 17tr, 18b, OBCtr. ticktock Media Archive: 10r, 15l, 19t, 20 OFCl,
OBC far right x3.
Every effort has been made to trace the copyright holders, and we apologise in advance for any
unintentional omissions. We would be pleased to insert the appropriate acknowledgements in
any subsequent edition of this publication.

Contents

Words in **bold** are explained in the glossary!

All in a day

We are going to the beach tomorrow. We will be there all day. A day is a long time. This is how I spend my time in a day.

Time to eat

Breakfast
A **day** starts in the **morning**.
I eat breakfast in the morning.

Lunch
The middle of the day is called **noon**.
At noon, it is time to eat lunch.

Dinner
When the **afternoon** is over, it is time for dinner. Dinner is the last big meal of the day.

Time to play

I get home from school in the afternoon. Then it is time to play! I like to build things with my wooden blocks.

Time to sleep

In the **evening** it starts getting dark outside. I know it is almost bedtime. I put on my pyjamas and brush my teeth. Then I go to bed and sleep through the **night**.

My day at the beach

I pull back the curtains. Look! The Sun is rising. It is going to be a bright, sunny day.

Morning

Mum thinks it is perfect weather for our day at the beach.

I eat cereal for breakfast and then I have an apple. I will need lots of energy for later.

Time to go

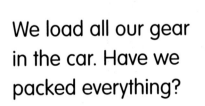

Let's find everything we need for swimming and playing. Don't forget the sun cream and sun hat. We need the car to carry all our gear.

We load all our gear in the car. Have we packed everything?

What do you take to the beach?

Morning at the beach

It takes an hour to get to the seaside. Mum keeps telling us we are nearly there.

When we arrive

We can smell the sea and hear the waves crashing. The Sun is getting really hot now.

Before we play, my sister, my brother and I must put on some sun cream.

Time for a splash

We splash in the sea. Mum and Dad join in. The water is cold. It makes my skin feel tingly.

Afterwards, we fly our kite.

Have you ever been to the seaside?

Noon at the beach

The Sun is high in the sky now. It is right above us! Dad says he feels hungry.

Time for lunch

Dad shows us his watch. We see that both hands on the watch are pointing at the 12. Dad says this time is 12 **o'clock** noon.

Mum says it is time to eat our sandwiches.

After lunch

When we finish our sandwiches, we build a sandcastle.

An **hour** later, Dad says we can go exploring. But first we have a cool drink and put on more sun cream.

Drinking a lot is important on hot days!

Afternoon at the beach

It is only 2 o'clock. We still have a lot of the afternoon left to explore and play.

Time to find out

We spend a long time looking for shells with Dad. There is so much to look at.

Hermit crabs have spiral shells.

This is a clam shell.

As we explore we leave everything as we find it.

Playtime

The Sun is not right over our heads any more,
butthe day still feels quite warm.

It is time for some tennis now
with Mum and Dad. Yippie!
My sister and I win two games.

What is your favourite game?

Almost time to go home

The Sun is getting lower in the sky and the air is feeling cooler. There is still time for some more beach fun!

One last swim

Mum says we have to go soon. But there is time for one last swim.

Quick! Let's run to the water. Swimming in the sea is fun. The water is much warmer now than it was this morning.

Time to pack up

Dad says it is 4 o'clock now. So we pack all our gear back in the car.

We are all really tired now, and a little bit hungry. It has been a busy day.

Make sure you don't leave any litter on the beach.

15

At home in the evening

By the time we get home, we are all really hungry. Mum promises us our favourite dinner...once we are clean!

Look at my feet!

The sand has stuck to the sun cream. It is in between my toes! This means it must be time for a shower.

Once we are clean it is time for some yummy dinner.

Dinner time

Fish with lots of vegetables is the best meal after a day at the beach. You can taste the sea in the fish! We eat our meal together and talk about our day at the beach.

The Sun is setting on the meadow behind our house. It is beginning to get dark. Dad says this time is called **dusk**.

What time do you have dinner?

Night time

After dinner my sister and I play a little. Then it is time to get ready for bed.

The Sun has set. The Moon is out and the stars are twinkling. It is night time now.

Ready for bed?

First we clean our teeth. After that we put on our pyjamas. Then we snuggle up in bed now that night is here.

Story time

Before I go to bed, Dad reads my favourite books to me about the beach and the ocean.

I wonder what my dreams will be after my day at the beach? Maybe they will be about building a sandcastle as big as a house!

What do you dream about?

Time facts

There are lots of things to learn about the time. How many of these facts do you know?

Days and weeks

Days of the week
There are seven days in the **week**.

Monday
Tuesday
Wednesday
Thursday
Friday
Saturday
Sunday

Each day has 24 hours.
Each day has daytime and night time. Daytime is made up of morning, noon, afternoon and evening.

Telling the time
Clocks and watches are used to tell the time of the day.

Months of the year

A **year** has 12 months.

January
February
March
April
May
June
July
August
September
October
November
December

Seasons

There are four seasons each year. These are spring, summer, autumn and winter.

spring

summer

autumn

winter

Which month is your birthday in?

What season is it now?

21

Time to remember

There have been lots of exciting things to learn about time in this book. How many can you remember?

What order do these words go in?

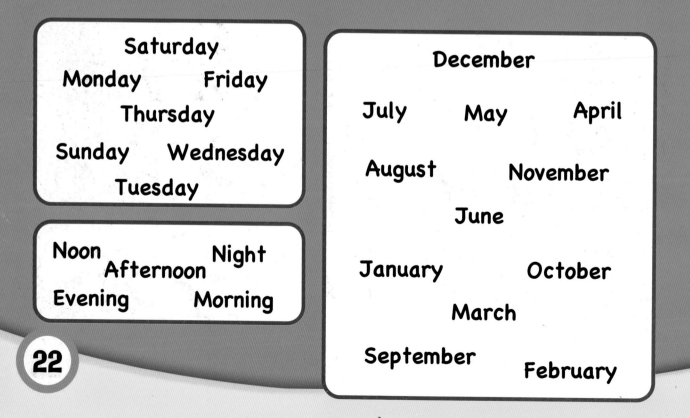

Saturday
Monday   Friday
Thursday
Sunday   Wednesday
Tuesday

Noon   Night
Afternoon
Evening   Morning

December
July   May   April
August   November
June
January   October
March
September   February

What part of the day?
Match the part of the day with the right pictures.

| Morning | Evening | Night | Noon |

What month is it now?

Glossary

Afternoon Afternoon is the time between noon, or 12 o'clock, and dinner time.

Day A day is 24 hours. It starts and ends at midnight. A day has daytime and night time. Daytime has four parts: morning, noon, afternoon and evening.

Dusk The time at the end of the day when the Sun is setting and the light is getting dim.

Evening Evening is the time between having your dinner and going to bed. Sometimes this is when the Sun is setting, too.

Hour An hour is 60 minutes. There are 24 hours in every day.

Minute A minute is 60 seconds. There are 60 minutes in every hour.

Morning The time between when you wake-up and noon.

Night The time when it is dark outside and you are in bed.

Noon The middle of the day. It is 12 o'clock. Sometimes it is called midday.

O'Clock This is used when telling the time. It tells you that the big minute hand is pointing exactly at the 12. The time is exactly the number the little hand is pointing at, such as 8 o'clock.

Week A week has seven days. They are Monday, Tuesday, Wednesday, Thursday, Friday, Saturday and Sunday.

Year Each year has 12 months. Each month is made up of about 4 weeks. A year has 4 seasons. They are spring, summer, autumn and winter.

Do you remember what the times on these clocks are?